Pam Wedgwood

AF084289

grades 3-4

Up-Grade!
Pop Piano

Light relief between the grades

Spaß und Entspannung mit leichten Stücken für Klavier Dritter Schwierigkeitsgrad
Plaisir et détente avec des pièces simples pour piano Niveau 3

Contents

#	Title	Artist/Source	Composer(s)	page
1.	**(Meet) the Flintstones**		Barbera/Hanna/Curtin	3
2.	**Mamma mia**	*Abba*	Andersson/Ulvaeus/Anderson	4
3.	**A whole new world**	*from Aladdin*	Rice/Menken	6
4.	**Electric dreams**		Wedgwood	8
5.	**How to save a life**	*The Fray*	King/Slade	10
6.	**Reach**	*S Club 7*	Dennis/Todd	12
7.	**Say you will**		Wedgwood	14
8.	**The circle of life**	*from The Lion King*	Rice/John	16
9.	**Patience**	*Take That*	Barlow/Orange/Donald/Owen/Shanks	18
10.	**Summer nights**	*from Grease*	Casey/Jacobs	20
11.	**Hey there Delilah**	*Plain White T's*	Higgenson	22

© 2008 by Faber Music Ltd
This edition first published in 2008
Bloomsbury House
74–77 Great Russell Street
London WC1B 3DA
Music processed by Don Sheppard
Cover design by Stik
Printed in England by Caligraving Ltd
All rights reserved

ISBN10: 0-571-53125-3
EAN13: 978-0-571-53125-7

To buy Faber Music publications or to find out about the full range of titles available
please contact your local music retailer or Faber Music sales enquiries:

Faber Music Limited, Burnt Mill, Elizabeth Way, Harlow CM20 2HX
Tel: +44 (0)1279 82 89 82   Fax: +44 (0)1279 82 89 83
sales@fabermusic.com   fabermusicstore.com

1. (Meet) the Flintstones

Words and Music by Joseph Barbera,
William Hanna and Hoyt Curtin

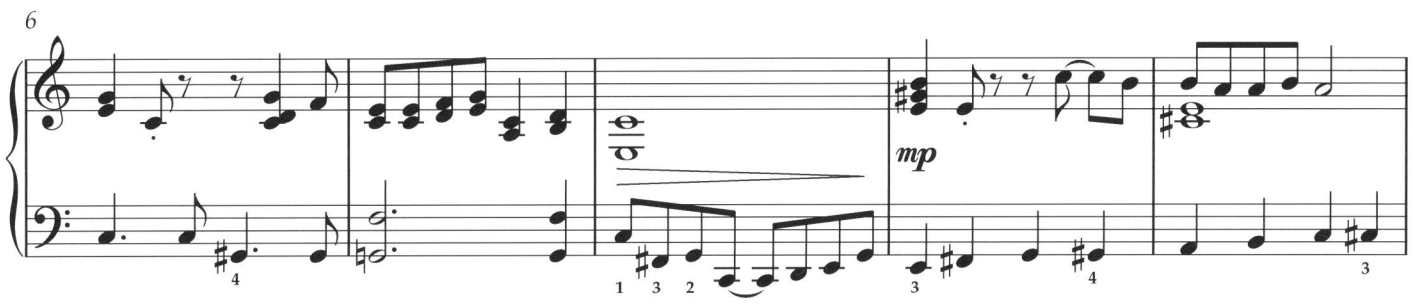

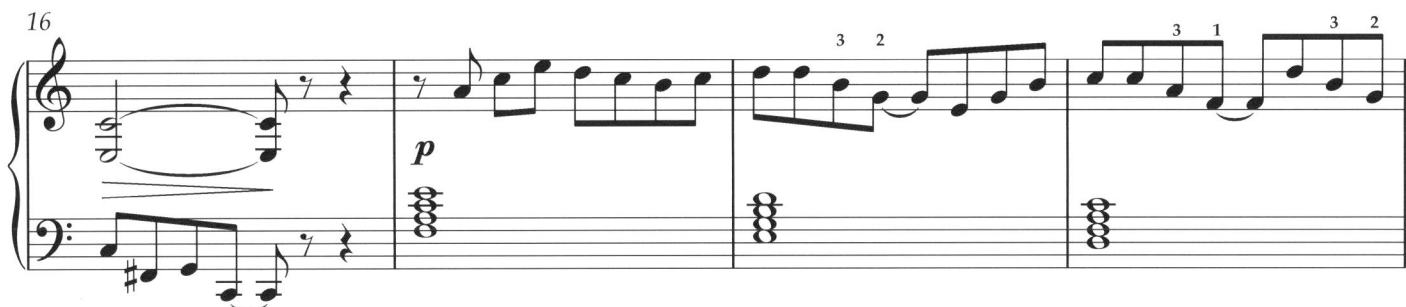
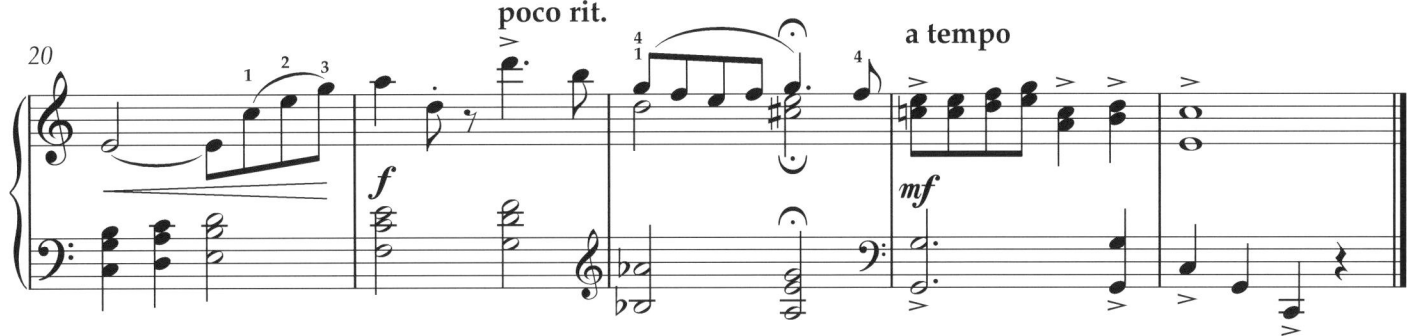

© 1960 Barbera-Hanna Music
EMI Music Publishing Ltd

This music is copyright. Photocopying is ILLEGAL and is THEFT.

2. Mamma mia

Words and Music by Benny Andersson,
Björn Ulvaeus and Stig Anderson

© 1975 Universal/Union Songs Musikforlag AS, Sweden
Bocu Music Ltd

3. A whole new world

from *Aladdin*

Words by Tim Rice
Music by Alan Menken

© 1992 Wonderland Music Co Inc and Walt Disney Music (USA) Co
Warner/Chappell Artemis Music Ltd

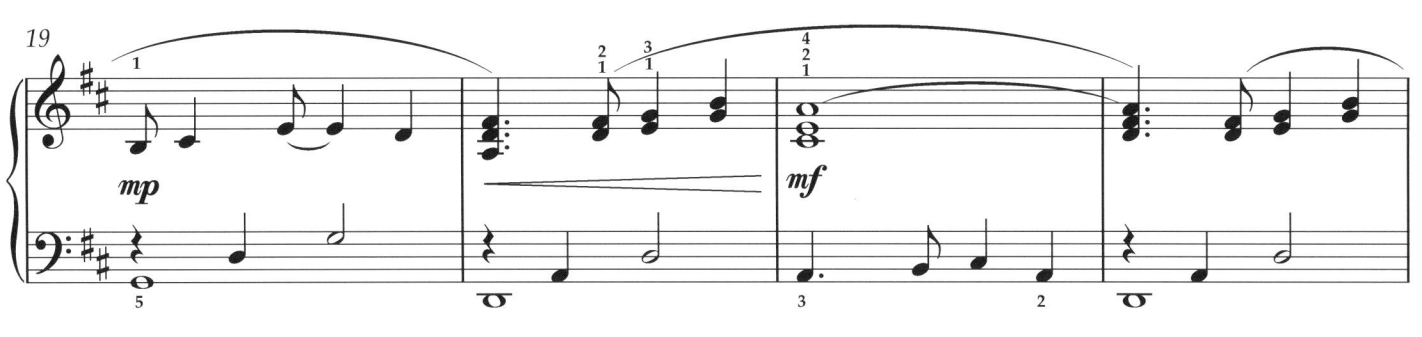
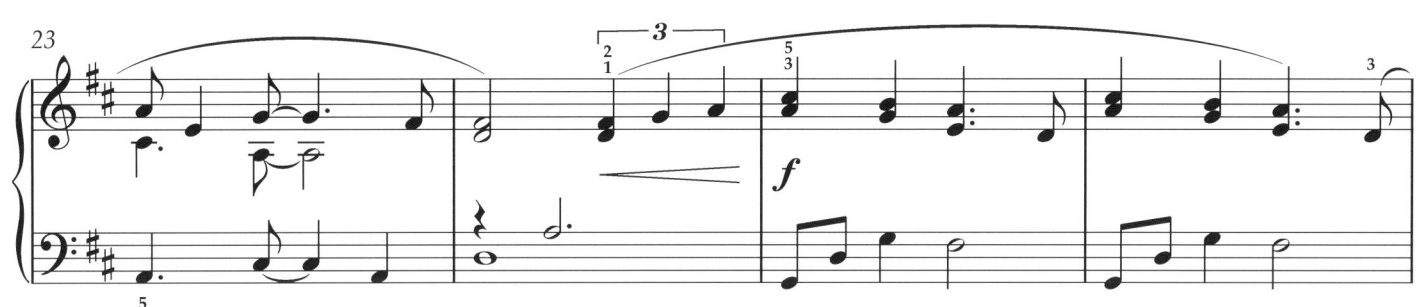
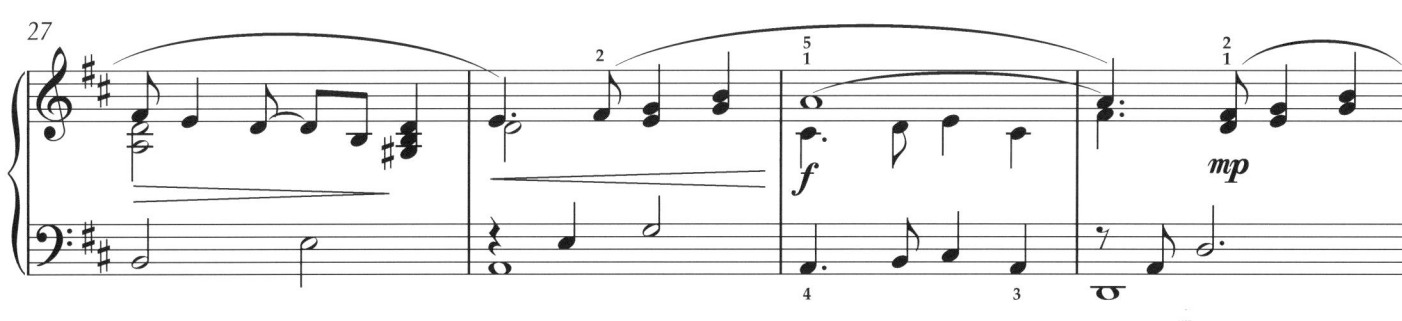

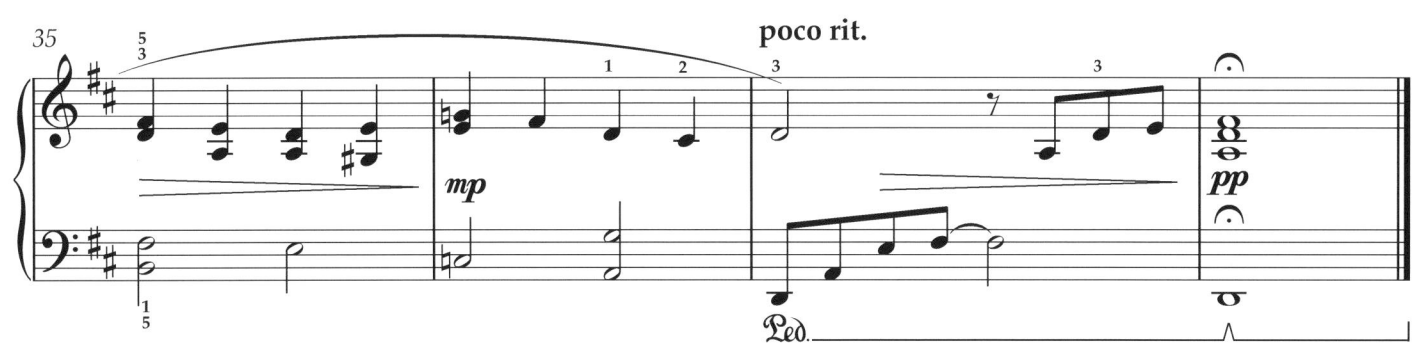

4. Electric dreams

Pam Wedgwood

Disco style with energy ♩ = 116

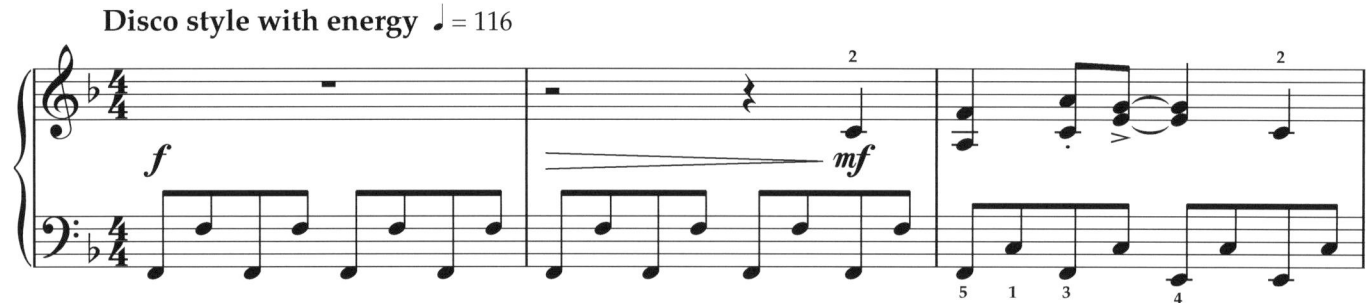
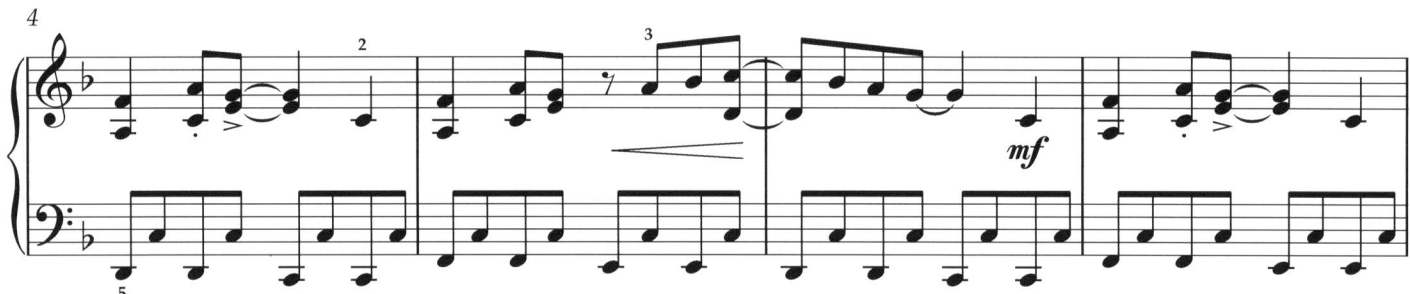

© 2008 by Faber Music Ltd

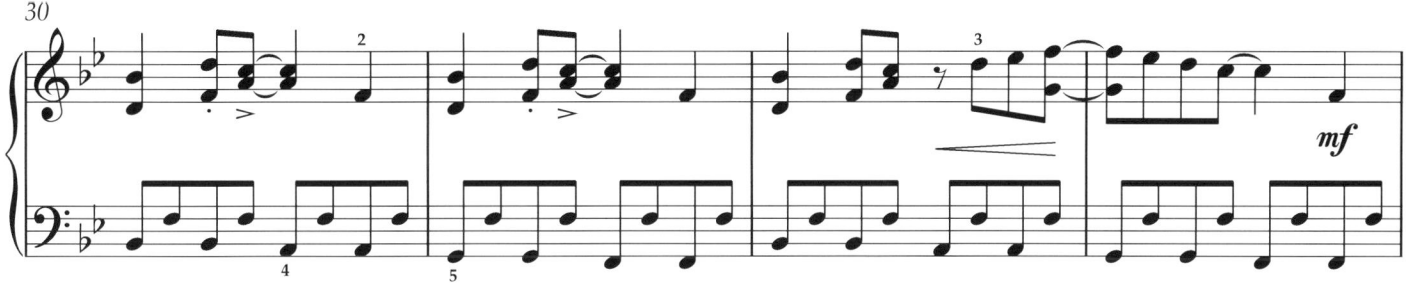
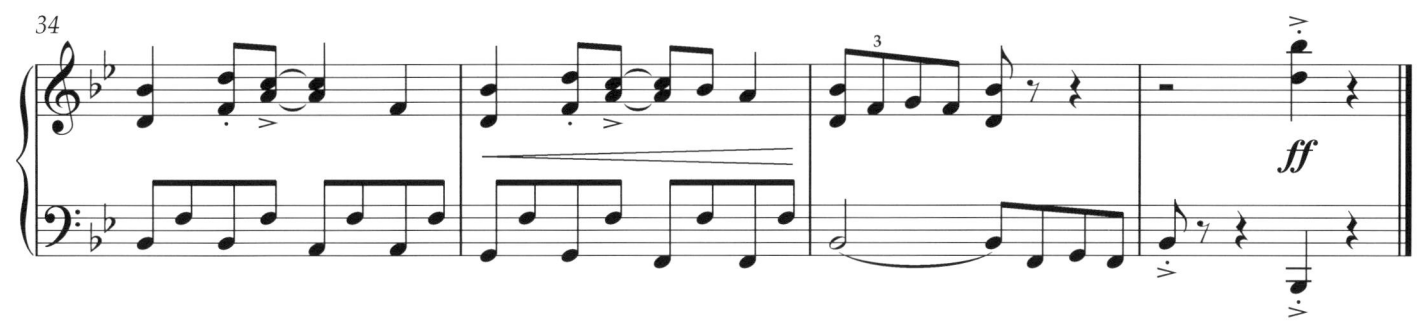

5. How to save a life

Words and Music by
Joseph King and Isaac Slade

© 2005 Aaron Edwards Publishing and EMI April Music Inc
EMI Music Publishing Ltd

6. Reach

Words and Music by
Cathy Dennis and Andrew Todd

© 2000 EMI Music Publishing Ltd and BMG Music Publishing Ltd

7. Say you will

Pam Wedgwood

8. The circle of life

from *The Lion King*

Words by Tim Rice
Music by Elton John

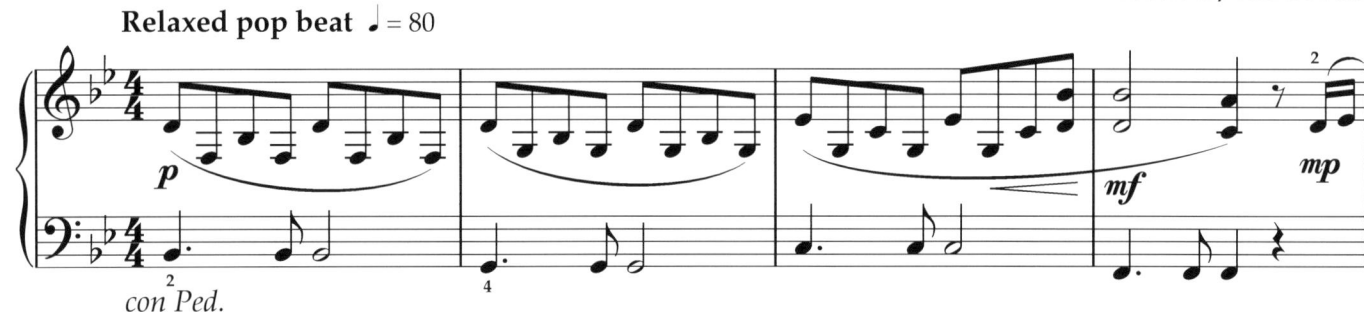

© 1994 Wonderland Music Company Inc
Warner/Chappell Artemis Music Ltd

9. Patience

Words and Music by Gary Barlow,
Jason Orange, Howard Donald,
Mark Owen and John Shanks

© 2006 EMI Music Publishing Ltd, Warner/Chappell North America Ltd,
BMG Music Publishing Ltd and Sony/ATV Music Publishing (UK) Ltd

10. Summer nights

from *Grease*

Words and Music by
Warren Casey and Jim Jacobs

Moderate rock speed ♩ = 108

© 1972 Edwin H Morris & Co Inc
Chappell Morris Ltd

11. Hey there Delilah

Words and Music by
Tom Higgenson

© 2005 Warner Bros Music Corp, Fear More Music and So Happy Publishing
Warner/Chappell North America Ltd